CONTENTS

Abbreviations **km** stands for kilometres • **m** stands for metres • **ft** stands for feet

The real Indiana Jones

Indiana Jones is real! Well, the character is made up but there are people like him looking for treasure all around the world. You can see some of their amazing finds in museums – and in this book!

If you just wandered around the world digging for treasure, you might find some broken china but not much else. These days, delving for valuables is a complicated business. Professional treasure hunters use modern technology, from satellites to microscopes, as well as treasure maps.

This gold knife from Peru is over 1,500 years old. It took a bit of polishing!

Made to last

Many old objects crumble away after just a few years. But treasures made of metal and gemstones are survivors – they take much longer to **decay** in air or water.

decay to slowly break down, or rot

4

Treasure Hunter

Discover Lost Cities and Pirate Gold

James de Winter

A & C Black • London

Produced for A & C Black by
Monkey Puzzle Media Ltd
48 York Avenue
Hove BN3 1JD, UK

Published by A & C Black Publishers Limited
36 Soho Square, London W1D 3QY

Paperback published 2010
First published 2009
Copyright © 2009 A & C Black Publishers Limited

ISBN 978-1-4081-1258-8 (hardback)
ISBN 978-1-4081-1993-8 (paperback)

Editor: Susie Brooks
Design: Mayer Media Ltd
Picture research: Lynda Lines
Series consultants: Jane Turner and James de Winter

This book is produced using paper that is made
from wood grown in managed, sustainable forests.
It is natural, renewable and recyclable. The logging
and manufacturing processes conform to the
environmental regulations of the country of origin.

Printed in Malaysia by Tien Wah Press (Pte.) Ltd

Picture acknowledgements
Alamy pp. 9 top (Kevin Schafer), 12 (The London
Art Archive), 16 (Ken Welsh), 17 (Danita Delimont),
23 (Mary Evans Picture Library); Art Archive pp. 1,
18–19 (Historiska Muséet Stockholm/Gianni Dagli
Orti); Corbis pp. 10 (Hulton Deutsch Collection),
19 top (Bettmann), 24–25 (Richard T Nowitz);
Getty Images pp. 4, 6 (Louis Grandadam), 7 (Digital
Globe), 11, 15 (AFP), 24 left (Matthew Wakem), 28
(AFP), 29 (Bridgeman Art Library); iStockphoto
p. 22 top (Deborah Cheramie); MPM Images p. 25
top; Rex Features pp. 5 (Paramount/Everett), 14
(Sipa Press), 26 top (Nils Jorgensen), 26–27 (Disney/
Everett); Science Photo Library pp. 20 (Institute of
Oceanographic Services/NERC), 21 (Klein Associates);
Topfoto.co.uk pp. 8–9 (AA World Travel Library),
13; Wikimedia Commons p. 22 bottom.

The front cover shows divers finding treasure on
the seabed (Corbis/Stephen Frink).

Every effort has been made to contact copyright
holders of material reproduced in this book. Any
omissions will be rectified in subsequent printings if
notice is given to the publishers.

In the films, Indiana Jones is an **archaeologist**.

Treasure hunting can be a scary business, especially if you're terrified of spiders.

Don't touch!
Archaeologists have to take care not to damage their ancient finds.

Did you bring a duster, Indie?

No — did you?

archaeologist someone who studies ancient peoples by looking at things they left behind

5

Clues from above

Who would have thought you could spot buried treasure from space? Amazingly, photos taken from aircraft or satellites can reveal secrets that we can't see from the ground.

The ruins of Palenque in Mexico are hidden in thick jungle and can only be spotted from a plane.

Satellites **orbiting** 800 kilometres (500 miles) above the Earth can zoom in on an object the size of this book! It is possible to tell where buildings once stood by looking at patterns in **aerial** and satellite photographs. For example, if grass looks a slightly different colour in some areas, it might mean there's something interesting underneath.

Ancient Big Apple

Satellite photos have shown that 500 years ago, Angkor (right) was about the size of New York City today.

orbit to circle or move around something, like Earth moves round the Sun

Satellite photos helped archaeologists to unearth the ruined city of Angkor in Cambodia. This is just part of it.

From space, a huge area can be pictured in one go.

Plants growing on top of buried rubble will not get enough water and **nutrients**.

Ground looks a different colour when seen from above.

On a hill in the middle is the temple of Angkor Wat.

This moat is 200 m (656 ft) wide – that's about the length of two football pitches!

aerial from the air or sky   **nutrients** things that plants need to grow and stay healthy

Mysteries of the mountains

It took a lot of puff to discover Machu Picchu! This "lost city of the Incas" stands almost 2,500 metres (8,200 feet) above sea level, in the mountains of Peru. Many people think it was a luxury holiday home rather than a city.

Hiram Bingham III was the first treasure hunter to visit the city in 1911. He recovered over 5,000 objects, including silver statues and valuable jewellery. He also discovered Inca stories written by tying knots in pieces of string. Bingham took many treasures home to the USA, where they remain to this day.

Solar system

The Sun and stars meant a lot to the Incas. They built giant sundials and star clocks that perfectly lined up with the Sun and stars on important days of the year.

Machu Picchu was built in around 1460. It may only have been used for about 100 years.

Incas people who created a vast kingdom in the Andes mountains of South America in the 1400s

This gold mask from Peru has lasted almost 1,000 years. Its coloured paint has faded, but the gold is still in perfect condition.

Some crop seeds lay **dormant**.

Terraces cut into the slopes made flat land for growing crops.

Dormant seeds can still be grown into healthy plants hundreds of years later!

dormant when the growth of a living thing slows or stops

9

Curse of the tomb

Anybody home?

When Howard Carter shone a candle into a dusty Egyptian doorway, he saw the gleam of gold. He was looking into the tomb of King Tutankhamun, who had once ruled ancient Egypt. Discovering King Tut's fabulous treasures made Carter famous.

"*Death Shall Come on Swift Wings to Him Who Disturbs the Peace of the King.*" This carving on the outside of Tutankhamun's tomb was feared as a curse – but it was just made up to keep thieves out.

Howard Carter opens the tomb in 1922, over 3,000 years after Tutankhamun died.

The Egyptians wanted their dead bodies to be kept in great condition. They wrapped them in cloth and used chemicals to preserve them. The result was called a mummy.

tomb a large building or chamber over someone's grave

Curse or poison?

Soon after Tutankhamun's tomb was opened, some of the workers died unexpectedly. Was it the curse? More likely, a poisonous **fungus** inside the mummy's wrapping made them ill.

Masks protect people unwrapping a mummy from poisoning.

Skin and flesh survive for a very, *very* long time.

The body is tightly wrapped.

AIR CANNOT GET IN.

fungus a living thing that can grow in the dark, such as mushrooms or mould

Buried in a boat

Who'd be mad enough to bury a boat in a field? It may seem silly, but many years ago being buried with your boat was a great honour.

In the 1930s, a mound at Sutton Hoo in Suffolk, England, was **excavated**. A whole boat, almost 30 metres (100 feet) long, was discovered inside. Long ago there would have been a body in it too. But tests showed that this had dissolved in the **acid** soil.

Archaeologists found many treasures inside the Sutton Hoo mound, including bowls, spoons, belt buckles, spears, swords and a shield.

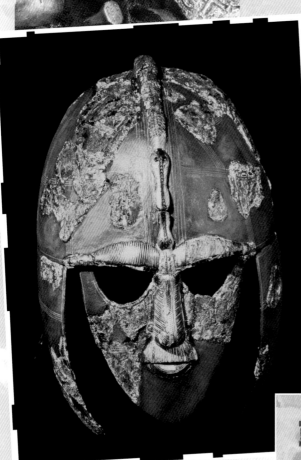

This burial helmet was rebuilt from hundreds of pieces.

Rust head

An iron helmet found at Sutton Hoo had **rusted** in the damp soil. Only four have ever been found in the UK.

excavate dig up   **acid** a type of chemical that can break down some materials

Hardly any of the original wood survived, but the boat's shape was still clear.

Burial chamber was in centre of ship.

The Sutton Hoo boat was probably buried in the 6th century AD.

Metal nails remain long after wood has rotted.

rust a non-reversible change that happens when iron objects are exposed to air and water

Fake finds

Don't believe everything you see! **Forgers** go to great efforts – perhaps even murder – to make objects look old and therefore worth lots of money.

Ape man

The famous British Piltdown man was meant to be a person from 500,000 years ago. In fact, it was a fake, made from a human skull plus the jaw of an orangutan.

In 2000, a mummified body in Pakistan caused great excitement. Lying in a carved stone coffin with a beautiful gold mask, it seemed to be a princess from over 2,500 years ago.

No one had ever seen anything like this before, and soon people got suspicious. Then **X-rays** showed that the woman had been dead for only a few years. Her neck had been broken. Had she been murdered? No one knows.

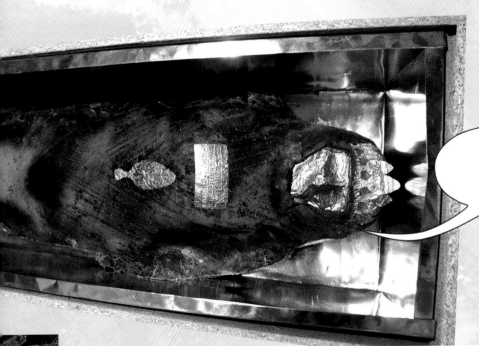

I'm a fake!

The mummy princess was a clever fake. It would have been worth millions if it had been real.

forgers people who make fake versions of valuable objects

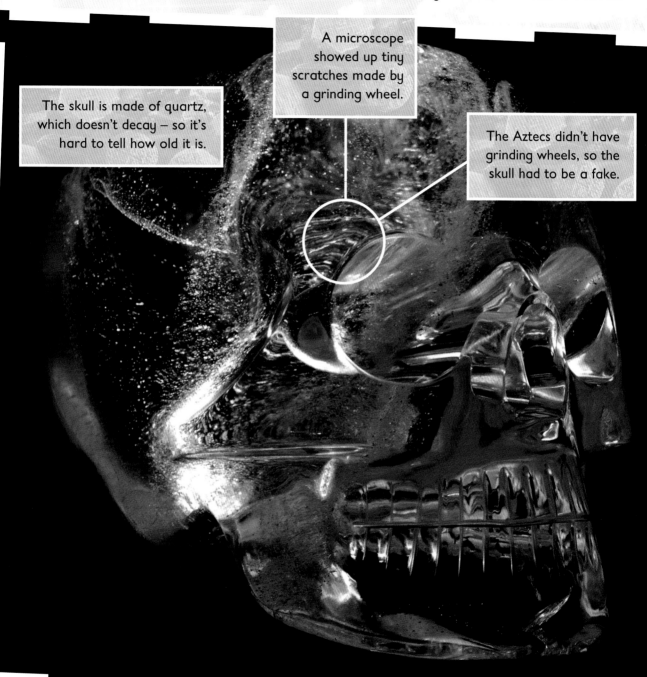

Nice try, but this crystal skull was NOT made by the ancient Aztecs of Mexico!

A microscope showed up tiny scratches made by a grinding wheel.

The skull is made of quartz, which doesn't decay — so it's hard to tell how old it is.

The Aztecs didn't have grinding wheels, so the skull had to be a fake.

X-rays special waves, a bit like radio waves, that can be used to see through objects

Secrets inside a mummy

A dead body can rot away very quickly. But if it's kept cold and away from air and water, a corpse may last for hundreds of years. Skin, bones, hair... they're all still there in a mummy!

Mummies can form naturally or be made by people. Before people wrap mummies, they sometimes remove inside bits such as the heart, brain and intestines. This slows down **bacteria** that cause decay. Injecting bodies with chemicals or covering them in wax are other ways to keep the dead bodies fresh.

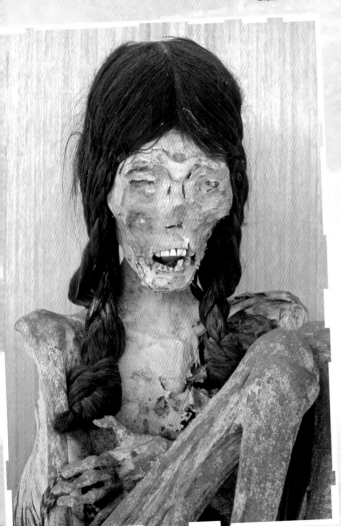

This mummy, known as "Miss Chile", still has her hair from 1,000 years ago.

bacteria tiny living things that eat away dead animals and plants

The boy king

Tutankhamun became pharaoh, or ruler, of ancient Egypt at 8 or 9 years old. He reigned for less than 10 years, and died when he was about 17.

*A **CT scan** looks inside Tutankhamun's mummy.*

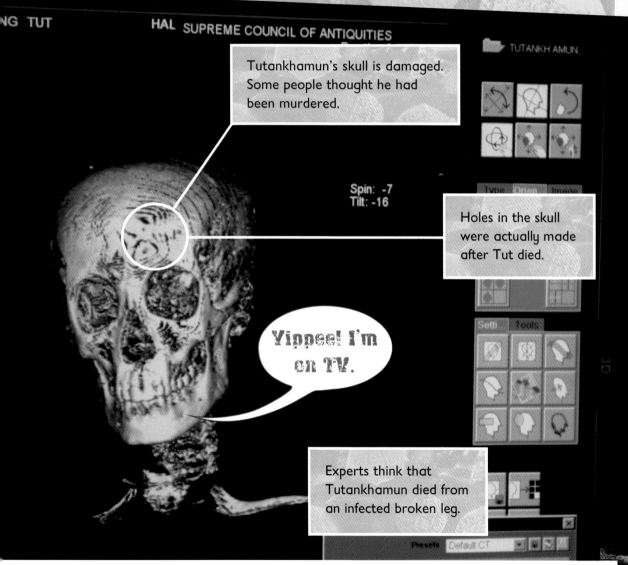

NG TUT   HAL   SUPREME COUNCIL OF ANTIQUITIES

TUTANKH AMUN.

Tutankhamun's skull is damaged. Some people thought he had been murdered.

Spin: -7
Tilt: -16

Holes in the skull were actually made after Tut died.

Type   Quan   Image

Seth   Tools

Yippee! I'm on TV.

Experts think that Tutankhamun died from an infected broken leg.

3D

Presets   Default CT

CT scan a special way of using X-rays and computers to scan a whole body

Viking valuables

The Vikings roamed the seas of Northern Europe, terrorising everyone they met and capturing treasures. They raided villages without warning, taking anything valuable and killing anyone who got in their way.

The Vikings loved jewellery — especially twisted bracelets and necklaces, called torques.

These gold and silver Viking treasures are 1,000 years old.

engineering using scientific ideas to design and make things

As well as being good with metals, the Vikings were great at **engineering**. They made some of the strongest boats in the ancient world.

The Vikings collected (and stole) coins like these from all over the world.

Gold and silver are rare and precious metals. They are soft and can be hammered and twisted easily into decorative shapes. One reason they stay shiny is because they don't normally **react** with the air or other chemicals around them.

Ancient Sat Nav

We know for certain that the Vikings used the stars to find their way. Some people think that they also used lodestones (magnetic rocks) as a kind of compass.

react to go through a chemical change

Seeing with sound

We use it to chat and bats use it to hunt for food, but sound can also help to find hidden treasure! Sound can get to places light cannot – and it travels through water.

You get a louder echo shouting at a wall than a pillow, because the hard wall bounces more sound waves back. The seabed is normally softer than a shipwreck, so by sending down sound waves, scientists can listen for the echo of any unusual hard objects.

The big orange object sends out sound waves, searching the seabed.

Ultra-clean

Ultrasound is used to clean delicate objects such as watches and jewellery without taking them apart. The sound waves "shake" off the dirt.

ultrasound sound waves that are too high-pitched for the human ear to hear

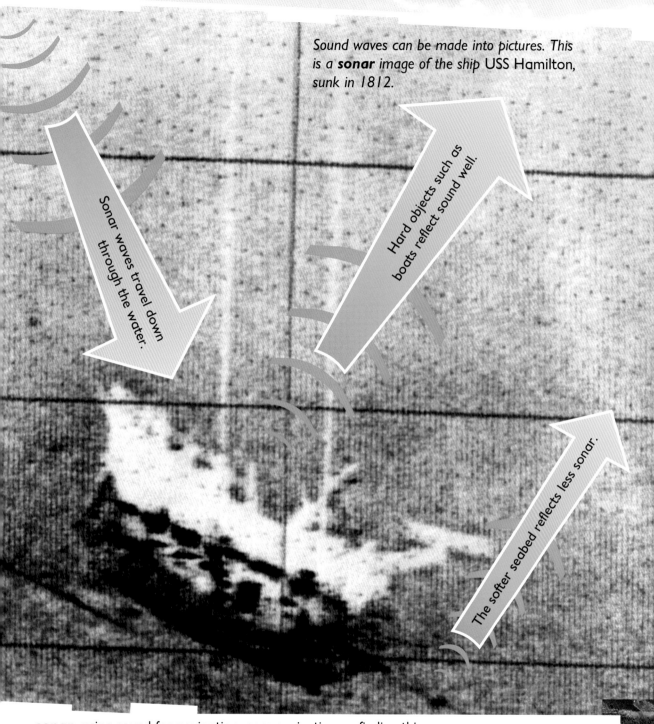

Sound waves can be made into pictures. This is a **sonar** image of the ship USS Hamilton, sunk in 1812.

Sonar waves travel down through the water.

Hard objects such as boats reflect sound well.

The softer seabed reflects less sonar.

sonar using sound for navigation, communication or finding things

Captain Kidd's hidden gold

Captain William Kidd was a real-life pirate. He was found guilty of piracy and murder, and hanged in 1701. Many people have tried to find the treasure he left behind.

If any of Kidd's treasure is still hidden somewhere, a mixture of detective work and science will help to find it. Sonar scanning and metal detectors can be used to search underground without a spade.

Is Kidd's treasure buried here on Gardiners Island, USA?

Modern pirates

Pirates still roam the seas today, using gadgets such as **GPS locators**, super-fast speedboats and high-powered weapons. Some ships try to scare them off by making high-pitched sounds with an **LRAD**.

Metal detectors use strong magnets to find buried metal objects.

GPS locator an electrical device that uses satellite signals to find a location

Captain Kidd buries his treasure in 1699. But where? People are still searching for it today.

Treasure included gold dust, bars of silver, Spanish doubloons, rubies, diamonds and candlesticks.

Chest didn't need to be airtight or waterproof – gold and gemstones do not rot.

LRAD long-range acoustic (sound) device

The Whydah Galley

One morning in 1717, "Black Sam" Bellamy spied a far-off ship. He raised his pirate flag, chased for three days and eventually captured the *Whydah*. Later that year, both the ship and its pirate crew sank in a howling storm.

Over 100,000 objects have been taken off the Whydah, including these Spanish coins and ring.

A thick crust of sand had to be cleaned off the treasures.

Barry Clifford spent 15 years searching for the Whydah.

The treasure included bars of solid gold.

The "X" on this old map shows where the Whydah was wrecked.

The *Whydah* is the only wrecked pirate ship ever found. It was said to be heavy with treasure stolen from more than 50 other ships.

Many of the objects from the *Whydah* are very delicate. Without careful treatment, they would have crumbled when taken out of the water.

Because gold doesn't react with water, the coins look as good as they did 300 years ago.

Even though they are completely soaked, many materials rot and decay much slower under the sea than they would in air.

Funny bone

One of the most amazing finds on the *Whydah* was a leg bone, which still had a shoe and sock on!

Titanic treasures

"Iceberg right ahead!" cries a voice through the cold, dark night. Two and a half hours later, over 1,500 people are dead and a mighty ship lies at the bottom of the Atlantic Ocean. Sunk in 1912, the *Titanic* must be the most famous shipwreck of all.

Many items recovered from the Titanic are in nearly perfect condition.

The iceberg made just six small gashes in the side of the *Titanic*, in total about the size of an unfolded newspaper. But these were enough to puncture some of the airtight sections that kept the boat afloat. As water rushed in through the gashes, the air rushed out – and the great *Titanic* went down.

The wreck is so far underwater that there is no natural light.

pressure how hard an object is being squeezed

Two wrecks!

When the *Titanic* was finally found after 70 years, it was in two parts. Massive forces had ripped it in two as it sank.

Some 4 km (2.5 miles) underwater, the Titanic is very difficult for scientists to work on.

The **pressure** from the water above is so high, a normal submarine would be crushed like a stamped-on drinks can.

A **submersible** lights up the deck of the *Titanic*.

submersible a small underwater vehicle connected to a boat or other submarine

Wreckers ashore

In the past, ships weren't only in danger at sea. Waiting on land were the wreckers, who would lure them on to the rocks to get hold of the treasures on board.

It's amazing what can wash up on a beach! Cargo like this has to be registered if you want to keep it.

On dark, stormy nights, wreckers stood by as the ships were smashed apart. Loads such as tobacco, tea and barrels of whisky or brandy have a **density** less than water, so they floated ashore.

density how closely packed something is

Long-distance light

The light bulbs used in modern lighthouses are not much stronger than a street light. But special **lenses** help the light to be seen up to 50 kilometres (30 miles) away.

Men would risk their lives to bring in goods from a wreck.

Sealed casks like this bobbed ashore.

Massive forces from crashing waves could wreck a boat in minutes.

lens a glass or plastic object designed to focus or change the direction of light

Glossary

acid a type of chemical that can break down some materials

aerial from the air or sky

archaeologist someone who studies ancient peoples by looking at things they left behind

bacteria tiny living things that eat away dead animals and plants

CT scan a special way of using X-rays and computers to scan a whole body

decay to slowly break down, or rot

density how closely packed something is

dormant when the growth of a living thing slows or stops

engineering using scientific ideas to design and make things

excavate a word used by archaeologists that means to dig up, record and study

forgers people who make fake versions of valuable objects

fungus a living thing that can grow in the dark, such as mushrooms or mould

GPS locator an electrical device that uses satellite signals to find a location

Incas people who created a vast kingdom in the Andes mountains of South America in the 1400s

lens a glass or plastic object designed to focus or change the direction of light

LRAD long-range acoustic (sound) device

nutrients things that plants need to grow and stay healthy

orbit to circle or move around something, like Earth moves round the Sun

pressure how hard an object is being squeezed

react to go through a chemical change

rust a non-reversible change that happens when iron objects are exposed to air and water

sonar using sound for navigation, communication or finding things

submersible a small underwater vehicle connected to a boat or other submarine

tomb a large building or chamber over someone's grave

ultrasound sound waves that are too high-pitched for the human ear to hear

X-rays special waves, a bit like radio waves, that can be used to see through objects

Further information

Books

Moonfleet by J. Meade Falkner (Penguin Popular Classics, 2007)
A popular children's book telling the story of John Trenchard, a 15-year-old boy who gets involved in smuggling and the search for Blackbeard's treasure.

King Solomon's Mines by H. Rider Haggard (Penguin Popular Classics, 2007)
A classic adventure story from the 19th century about an expedition in Africa.

Treasure Island by Robert Louis Stevenson (Penguin Popular Classics, 2007)
Perhaps the most famous pirate treasure story ever.

Films

Raiders of the Lost Ark directed by Steven Spielberg (Paramount Pictures, 1981)
One of a series of adventure films about the archaeologist/treasure hunter Indiana Jones.

Pirates of the Caribbean: The Curse of the Black Pearl directed by Gore Verbinski (Walt Disney Company, 2003)
Join Captain Jack Sparrow as he leads the *Black Pearl* and a band of pirates to find Aztec gold and adventure.

National Treasure directed by Jon Turteltaub (Buena Vista Pictures, 2004)
A treasure hunter tries to track down treasure lost for centuries. Lots of maps, codes, secret passages and mysteries are involved.

Websites

http://whydah.com
Information, photographs and links connected with the wreck of the *Whydah*.

www.shipwreckcenter.org
Lots of details about various shipwrecks around the world, including a section on real pirates.

www.egyptianmuseum.gov.eg
Full details and images of many Egyptian treasures, including those from the tomb of Tutankhamun.

Index